Ted Shuttlesworth

The Road to Healing

Where does faith for healing come from?

How can I be healed?

How to keep your healing?

Unless otherwise indicated, all Scripture quotations are from the King James Version of the Bible.

The Road to Healing
ISBN-13:978-0-9789883-4-0
ISBN-10:0-9789883-4-5
Printed in the United States of America

Copyright © 2007 by Ted Shuttlesworth

Published by T.S.E.A., Inc.
P. O. Box 7
Farmington, West Virginia 26571
www.tedshuttlesworth.com

All rights reserved. Contents and / or cover may not be reproduced in whole or in part in any form without the express written consent of the publisher.

This study on healing is dedicated to my family who have always supported me; and to Sherry who keeps the Ministry Office running smoothly, to Misty who helped with the editing of the manuscript, and all of my staff who are a part of the healing ministry of Jesus Christ.

Brother Bob,

Thank you for your ministry of faithfulness. The best is yet to come!

304·657·0019 cell
287·2943 home

HEB. 11:6

Foreword

God is a good God. He's completely and absolutely good. And God wants good for us. God tells us this in *III John 2*, "Beloved, I wish above all things that thou mayest prosper and be in health even as thy soul prospereth."

God wants His children to be whole and healthy - mind, soul AND body.

Nearly everybody in the world is sick in someway and needs healing. Healing is for the total person - his mind, his soul, and his body. In Matthew 4:23, we learn that Jesus' mission was three-fold. We're told that He went about all Galilee, teaching to the mind, preaching to the soul and HEALING of the body. Jesus spent two thirds of His ministry healing the people so they could have good health.

THE ROAD TO HEALING focuses on this oft forgotten third mission of Christ. The provision of the Cross reveals that healing is not only our privilege, it is our right.

Friend, I know that I know that I know, this book will give you fresh revelation and I believe that something good is going to happen to YOU today.

Oral Roberts

Introduction

There is a Biblical road that you must travel to receive healing from the Lord. It is a journey from sickness to health.

There are many hurting people who have never heard the oldest story of help and healing. It is the oldest story because it is based on He who is Alpha. It is the last word on healing no matter how many modern cures remain yet to be discovered, for He is Omega. The beginning of your journey to health and the end of your healing quest is found in the person of Jesus Christ!

> **"I am Alpha Omega, the beginning and the ending, saith the Lord, which is , and which was, and which is to come, the Almighty."**
> **(Revelation 1:8)**

Isaiah looked through God's telescope and saw through the ages to come. He,

> **".....which is, and which was, and which is to come....."**
> **(Revelation 1:8)**

And this Old Testament prophet wrote:

> "Surely, he hath borne our griefs, and carried our sorrows: yet we did esteem him stricken, smitten of God, and afflicted.

> **But he was wounded for our transgression, he was bruised for our iniquities: the chastisement of our peace was upon him; and with his stripes we are healed."**
>
> **(Isaiah 53:4,5)**

The fulfillment of this prophecy is found in the eighth chapter of Matthew. The telescope focused in on the human drama of Suffering's meeting with Heaven's Healing Balm.

Matthew, chapter eight, is the healing chapter of the New Testament. It is in this chapter that the prophecy of Isaiah 53 finds its actual fulfillment.

Contents

chapter one
"God Wants You to be Healed" 1

chapter two
"How to Receive Healing" 9

chapter three
"The Ministry of the Laying on of Hands" 22

chapter four
"How to Keep Your Healing" 29

chapter one

"God Wants You to be Healed"

"When he was come down from the mountain, great multitudes followed him.

And, behold, there came a leper and worshipped him, saying, Lord, if thou wilt, thou canst make me clean.

And Jesus put forth his hand, and touched him, saying, I will; be thou clean. And immediately his leprosy was cleansed."
                                              (Matthew 8:1-3)

Jesus is always ready and willing to touch the untouchable. The leper risked his life to find the answer to this question. *"Is it your will Jesus for lepers to be healed?"*

Faith for healing begins with God's Word. The leper was listening for Jesus' word. Yes, meant hope and health! No, meant disease and death!

Jesus said,

"I will; be thou clean."
                                              (Matthew 8:3)

Two words created faith in the leper's heart.

Two words spelled the end of a lonely life.

Two words stopped the spread of a dreaded disease.

The Road to Healing

Two words ended the suffering in this man's flesh.

Two words released faith in the heart of the seeker.

"I WILL". When the "I AM" says "I WILL", all Heaven shouts while hell cries and earth is made glad!

It is never God's will for you to be sick! God is not the Author of your sickness. He is not redeeming you through allowing a disease to destroy you. You are redeemed through the blood that Jesus shed for you on the old rugged cross on Golgotha's brow, some two thousand years ago!

> **"But if we walk in the light, as He is in the light, we have fellowship one with another, and the blood of Jesus Christ his Son cleanseth us from all sin."**
>
> **(I John 1:7)**

> **"For all have sinned, and come short of the glory of God;**
>
> **Being justified freely by his grace through the redemption that is in Christ Jesus:**
>
> **Whom God hath set forth to be a propitiation through faith in his blood, to declare his righteousness for the remission of sins that are past, through the forbearance of God;"**
>
> **(Romans 3:23-25)**

FAITH IN HIS BLOOD! Faith does not come through some filthy tumor or cancer eating the life out of your flesh. God is not using some foul disease or affliction to chastise you as His child. God is not sending sickness upon this world to work out *"righteousness"* in their lives. Righteousness comes through faith in His blood!

There are those who teach a *"limited atonement"* when it comes to the work of the cross. These false teachers of religion have doomed whole generations to suffer under the guise of *"God is working out some mysterious good"*.

The blood of Jesus is enough! You are not made *"more holy"* or *"more spiritual"* by disease. It is not Calvary and cancer. It is not the atonement and arthritis. It is not faith and fever!

The holy blood of Jesus, all by itself is enough to cover all your sin. Faith in His blood is enough to make you righteous and give you right-standing with God. Calvary covers it all!

THE TRUE CROSS

When I was a young teenage preacher, I remember reading a book that contained an old legend of how that even the cross that Jesus died on brought healing and deliverance.

The story was told of how the mother of one of the emperors set out on a pilgrimage to Jerusalem. When she reached that Holy City, she gave instructions to find the cross that Jesus was crucified on.

Her men went to the foot of Golgotha and began to rum-

The Road to Healing

mage through the piles of rubbish, in hopes of finding His cross. They were surprised when their search revealed three crosses! However, the inscription which was placed over the head of Jesus was lying in a different place from where the crosses were.

They did not know which cross was the real cross. They gathered together all the sick and diseased and afflicted that they could find. They brought them to one cross and had them touch it, but nothing happened. They took them to another cross. When they tried it, the blind eyes were opened, deaf ears came unstopped, the lame leaped for joy, the sick were made whole. They had found the true cross!

Thank God for the Cross! God used the death of Christ to bring life to you, both spiritually and physically.

God is not the author of your sickness. If God is willing for one to be made whole of their disease, He is willing that all should be made whole. If not, then one can only assume that God has favored one over another. Yet, the Bible teaches that God is no respecter of people. He loves us all the same! Whether you are rich or poor, black or white, a man or a woman, young or old, sick or well, God loves you.

"Then Peter opened his mouth, and said, of a truth I perceive that God is no respecter of persons:"
(Acts 10:34)

"For God so loved the world, that He gave His only begotten son, that whosoever believeth in him should not perish, but have everlasting

life."
(John 3:16)

God loves humanity. He is not adding to the suffering of souls. He is not using dreaded diseases as "*love tokens*" from Heaven to "*bless*" mankind.

"........for God is love,"
(I John 4:8)

"Do not err, my beloved brethren. Every good gift and every perfect gift is from above, and cometh down from the Father of lights, with whom is no variableness, neither shadow of turning."
(James 1:16,17)

Sickness is not a good gift. It brings death and destruction when there is no cure. If, as some contend, that sickness can sometimes be God working out a Divine purpose, then would not those who believe such nonsense be fighting the will of God by using medicines and doctors to get well? Would it not be better to stay sick for His glory? Then, what happens if the doctor's administrations or the medicine brings a cure? Are the natural powers of man greater than the works of God? No, God is not the author of sickness or disease and He is not using your sickness to "*redeem*" you.

Sickness is never a work of God. The coming of Jesus was the beginning of the end of rampant destruction through sin, sickness and death.

> "...For this purpose the son of God was manifested, that He might destroy the works of the devil."
>
> **(I John 3:8)**
>
> "How God anointed Jesus of Nazareth with the Holy Ghost and with power: who went about doing good, and healing all that were oppressed of the devil; for God was with him."
>
> **(Acts 10:38)**

Jesus came to destroy the destroyer. Satan is the Apollyon (destroyer) of Revelation 9:11. Jesus said concerning this conflict of the ages:

> "The thief cometh not, but for to steal, and to kill, and to destroy: I am come that they might have life, and that they might have it more abundantly."
>
> **(John 10:10)**

Here, we have the mission of Satan and the mission of the Good Shepherd revealed; Death and life, robbery and abundance. Sickness is an oppression of Satan. It steals your health from you. It is Satan, the murderer, at work. It is incipient death.

Healing is God's anointing upon Jesus for all that are sick. It is the dynamic power of the Holy Ghost in explosions of deliverance. It is God with you. It is God, *"the Lord that healeth thee."* It is the Holy Ghost, *"The Paracletos,"* the One called alongside to help. It is Jesus, the Healer of humanity. Three

"God Wants You to be Healed"

have become one to bless and do good!

When Jesus opened the eyes of the blind, caused the deaf to hear, and made the lame to walk, the people testified that it was good.

> **"And were beyond measure astonished, saying, He hath done all things well: he maketh both the deaf to hear, and the dumb to speak."**
> **(Mark 7:37)**

It is a good thing to heal the sick and make the afflicted whole. Conversely, it is a bad thing, if not an evil thing, to make people sick or afflict them. Moses declared sickness to be an evil thing!

> **".......the evil diseases of Egypt,"**
> **(Deuteronomy 7:15)**

James taught the early church that God does not *"tempt"* or *"test"* His children with evil.

> **"Let no man say when he is tempted, I am tempted of God: For God cannot be tempted with evil, neither tempteth he any man."**
> **(James 1:13)**

The Bible says sickness is an evil thing. (Deuteronomy 7:15) God does not use evil to test any man. (James 1:13)

Jesus was anointed to destroy the works of the devil. (Acts 10:38, I John 3:8) Sickness is an oppression of the devil (Acts 10:38). The people who saw Jesus heal said that He had

The Road to Healing

done well. (Mark 7:37) The leper found out that it was Jesus' will for him to be made whole. (Matthew 8:3) Peter taught that God is no respecter of persons. (Acts 10:34)

WHAT GOD WILL DO FOR ONE: HE WILL DO FOR ALL!

IT IS GOD'S WILL FOR YOU, TOO, TO BE WHOLE!

The first signpost on the road to healing reads. "I WILL" make no mistake here friend. Jesus is willing to make you whole. It is the will of God for you to be healed!

Faith comes by hearing! When Jesus said, *"I will"*, the leper now had access to the miracle-working power of God. FAITH IS NOT A NATURAL FORCE! FAITH IS THE ABILITY OF GOD REVEALED! MAN CANNOT! GOD CAN! IT IS THE SCRIPTURE DEFINED.

> "...with men this is impossible; but with God all things are possible."
> (Matthew 19:26)

chapter two

"How to Receive Healing"

"And when Jesus was entered into Capernaum, there came unto him a centurion, beseeching him,

And saying, Lord, my servant lieth at home sick of the palsy, grievously tormented.

And Jesus saith unto him, I will come and heal him.

The centurion answered and said, Lord, I am not worthy that thou shouldest come under my roof: but speak the word only, and my servant shall be healed.

For I am a man under authority, having soldiers under me: and I say to this man, Go and he goeth; and to another, Come, and he cometh; and to my servant, Do this, and he doeth it.

When Jesus heard it, he marvelled, and said to them that followed, Verily I say unto you, I have not found so great faith, no, not in Israel."

(Matthew 8:5-10)

The Road to Healing

The greatest faith comes through understanding the authority of God's Word! There is no experience that is above the Word of God. There is no sickness that is greater than the Word of God.

"He sent His word, and healed them."
(Psalms 107:20)

The centurion recognized the authority that was in the words of Jesus. The Word of God is the vehicle that carries your healing to you. This transportation system never fails.

While travelling on the railroad from London to Gatwick airport, I saw a train that had derailed. The newspapers declared several had been killed. They never reached their final destination. God's Word always reaches its destination and it will always accomplish that which God has intended.

"So shall my word be that goeth forth out of my mouth: it shall not return unto me void, but it shall accomplish that which I please, and it shall prosper in the thing whereto I sent it."
(Isaiah 55:11)

The centurion knew that the beginning of his servant's healing was the Word of the Lord! All healing starts with the Word of God.

WHERE FAITH COMES FROM

"So then faith cometh by hearing, and hearing by the word of God."
(Romans 10:17)

"How to Receive Healing"

Where you go to church is important! What you hear preached is vital! Billy Sunday said, *"Going to church no more saves you than sitting in a garage makes you a car!"* We might paraphrase that by saying; *"Going to a church will no more heal you than sitting in a garage will make you a car!"*

Your church or your pastor may not believe in Divine healing. Since everything we receive from God is based upon faith, it does make a difference where you go to church and what you hear preached. Separate yourself from unbelief.

"Having a form of godliness, but denying the power thereof: from such turn away."
(II Timothy 3:5)

Some years ago, I had erected a tent in one of the greater cities of America. Night by night, God performed wonderful miracles when we prayed in the name of Jesus.

One night in particular, they brought to me a young boy born deaf and dumb. They call them deaf mutes. My father-in-law stood by my side and he and I agreed that God would perform the miracle.

I commanded the deaf and dumb spirits to go and never return, in the name of Jesus. Instantly, that boy heard and began to make sounds for the first time in his life. It was a wonderful miracle. I instructed the parents to teach him how to speak and our hearts were thrilled for them.

The Road to Healing

I had that tent up for almost two weeks. Sundays we encouraged the people to go to their own churches and I preached for the sponsoring church.

The Monday night after the first weekend, a woman approached me and my wife as we drove up behind the tent. I recognized her as the woman who had brought the boy who had been deaf and dumb. She told me a story that I have never forgotten. Apparently, when the parents went to their church on Sunday, they told the pastor of the great miracle that God had done. When the pastor heard it he replied. *"God did not heal your boy in that tent!" "No, he is healed, pastor, come see"*, they told him, but that pastor would not believe. Later, during the service, he told the congregation that God was not performing miracles in that tent meeting and he forbid his people to go the next week. (Completely ignoring the young boy who sat in the service) The mother then told us that same pastor was out in front of the tent with a notebook, writing down all the names of his people who were there that night. he was going to throw them out of the church if they came.

The mother told us one more thing that brought me great joy. She said that when they went home on Sunday, the boy let them know that when that preacher stood to preach, he could not hear one word that the minister said, even though he could hear all the other noises around him! God certainly has a sense of humor. I am convinced that there are certain so-called *"ministers"* whom God does not want us to hear. I tell people, *"find a church that is red hot, where they preach the full gospel."*

"How to Receive Healing"

Many in the church world today are missing God's instruction in this area. Instead of finding others of like precious faith and fellowshipping with them, some have said, *"Well, I'll just stay in my old church and try to change them."* If God has not been able to change many of these traditional churches who reject His power, what makes you think you are going to be able to change them? Separate yourself from unbelief.

The centurion was not a part of the *"household of Israel"* but Jesus said that his faith was the greatest faith in all of Israel. This was the greatest faith Jesus had ever seen.

THE GREATEST FAITH

Why did the centurion have the greatest faith Jesus had ever seen? The centurion was a soldier. Apparently, he was a compassionate man. He cared for his servant. The Bible shows us that he showed kindness to the Jews of Capernaum. He paid for the construction of a synagogue for them. This man was not the typical oppressor of the poor. Rome ruled with a heavy hand. Yet, this man cared for his servant and with kindness, served his community through the expense of a house for God and his people. What made his faith the greatest in all of the New Testament? HE UNDERSTOOD AUTHORITY!

"For I am a man under authority."
(Matthew 8:9)

"Where the word of the King is, there is power..."
(Ecclesiastes 8:4)

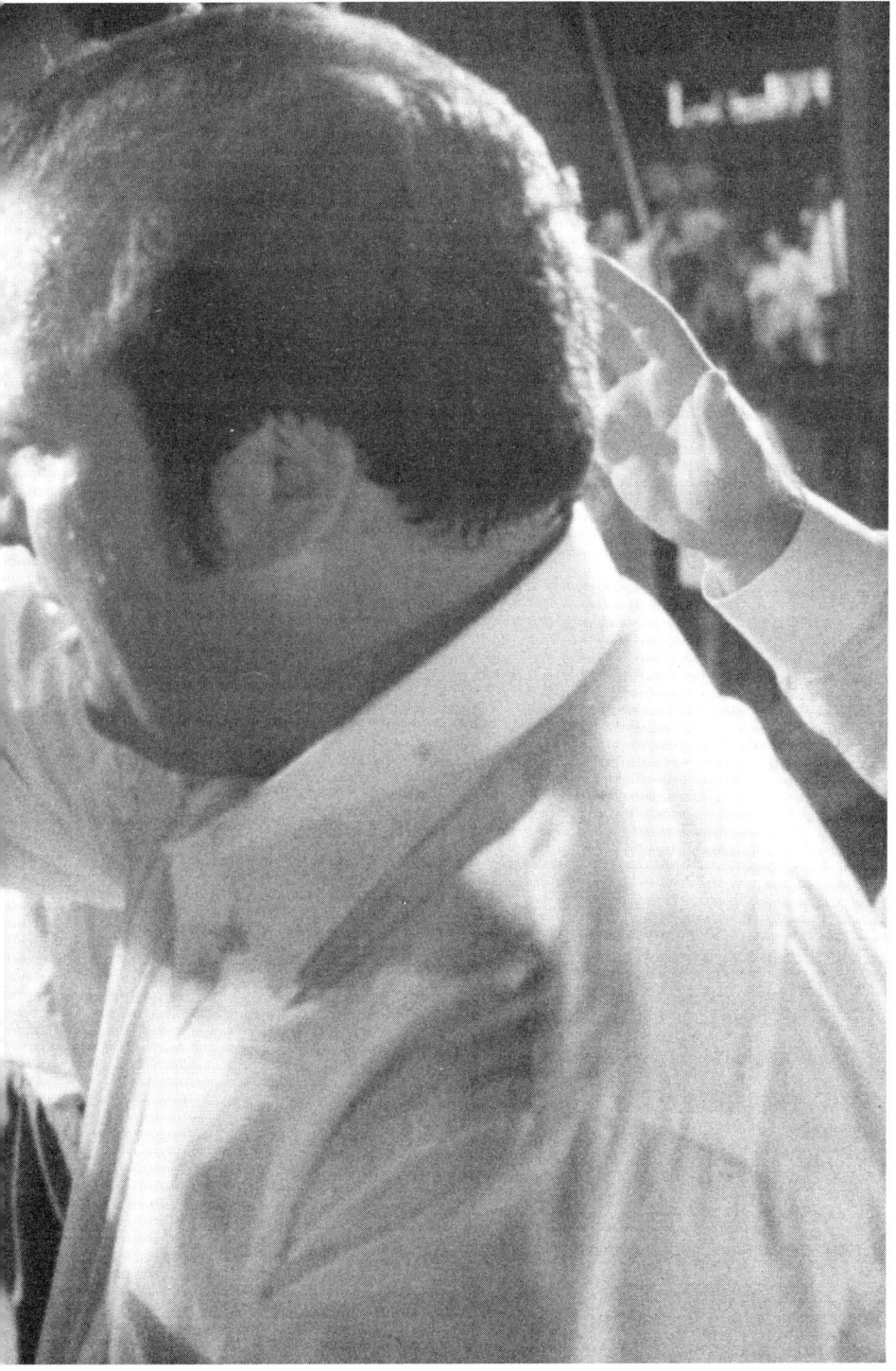

The Road to Healing

The Word and authority are synonymous. The centurion was not the only one that recognized this authority in the words of Jesus.

> "And they were astonished at his doctrine; for his word was with power."
>
> (Luke 4:32)

> "And they were all amazed, and spake among themselves, saying, What a word is this! For with authority and power he commandeth the unclean spirits, and they come out."
>
> (Luke 4:36)

> "He taught them as one having authority, and not as the scribes."
>
> (Matthew 7:29)

There are two words that are very important in understanding the difference between *"authority"* and *"power"*.

The word *"power"* in Luke 4:36 is the Greek word *"dunamis"*.

It is the same word in Acts 1:8:

> "But ye shall receive power, after that the Holy Ghost is come upon you: and ye shall be witnesses unto me both in Jerusalem, and in all Judaea, and in Samaria, and unto the uttermost part of earth."
>
> (Acts 1:8)

"How to Receive Healing"

Dunamis is the word from which we get our word, **dynamite**. Power! It signifies ability, might, of mighty works and miracles.

The second word is *"authority"* in Luke 4:36. It comes from the Greek word, *"exousia"*. This word means *"the right to act"*.

This was the basis of the centurion's faith. Literally, he said, *"Jesus, you have the right to make my servant whole, just by saying so!"* If that was true in that day, it is still true today.

> **"Jesus Christ the same yesterday, and today, and forever."**
> **(Hebrews 13:8)**

The word contains the seed for healing. When Jesus spoke, literally that word or words spoken, contained within them the right to make it happen! The centurion, who himself was a man of authority and under authority, recognized this principle in the ministry of Jesus. The centurion concluded; *"If I can just get Jesus to say that my servant is healed, he will be all right!"*

> **"... but speak the word only, and my servant shall be healed."**
> **(Matthew 8:8)**

The Road to Healing

Jesus taught this principle to His disciples by parable:

THE PARABLE OF THE SOWER

"And he taught them many things by parables, and said unto them in his doctrine.

Hearken; Behold, there went out a sower to sow:

And it came to pass, as he sowed, some fell by the way side, and the fowls of the air came and devoured it up.

And some fell on stony ground, where it had not much earth; and immediately it sprang up, because it had no depth of earth:

But when the sun was up, it was scorched; and because it had no root, it withered away.

And some fell among thorns, and the thorns grew up, and choked it, and it yielded no fruit.

And other fell on good ground, and did yield fruit that sprang up and increased; and brought forth, some thirty, and some sixty, and some hundred.

And he said unto them, He that hath ears to hear, let him hear.
(Mark 4:2-9)

Jesus taught in parables to *"them that were without"*. However, to you and I who are His disciples; *"...it is given to know the mystery of the kingdom of God:"* This parable of the sower and the seed is the parable which is the foundation to understanding all the other parables that Christ taught.

> **"And he said unto them, Know ye not this parable? and how then will ye know all parables?"**
> **(Mark 4:13)**

The parable of the sower then is the key to all parables and it is also the foundation for all healing. Freedom from sickness comes from knowing the truth. Remember this scripture?

> **"Sanctify them through thy truth: thy word is truth."**
> **(John 17:17)**

The word sanctify, means separate. God's Word will separate you from sin, sickness and death.

> **"And ye shall know the truth, and the truth shall make you free."**
> **(John 8:32)**

Somehow the centurion unlocked the door that brought healing. When Jesus would speak the word, that word was truth. No matter the illness or disease of his servant, the healing word became the truth; the disease became the lie! No matter the symptoms or apparent condition, the word of authority overruled! Hallelujah! Fenton's translation of Psalms 107:20 says: **"He sent His word, and It healed them."**

THE HEALING SEED

"Now the parable is this: The seed is the word of God."

(Luke 8:11)

A farmer will not receive a harvest until he plants a seed. The seed is powerless until it is planted. The first thing that God tells us about *"seed"* is in the Book of Beginnings.

"And God said, Behold, I have given you every herb bearing seed, which is upon the face of all the earth, and every tree, in the which is the fruit of a tree yielding seed; to you it shall be for meat."

(Genesis 1:29)

God gives the seed! Isaiah records:

"For as the rain cometh down, and the snow from heaven, and returneth not thither, but watereth the earth, and maketh it bring forth and bud, that it may give seed to the sower, and bread to the eater:

So shall my words be that goeth forth out of my mouth:"

(Isaiah 55:10,11)

"How to Receive Healing"

The seed is the word of God! Now, here is the foundation for our healing. Here is how healing comes to our bodies. The centurion knew it and said:

> **"...speak the word only, and my servant shall be healed."**
> **(Matthew 8:8)**

The Word is seed. When spoken, it is planted. Preachers, you get what you preach!

> **"But what saith it? The word is nigh thee, even in thy mouth, and in thy heart: that is, the word of faith, which we preach;"**
> **(Romans 10:8)**

> **"How then shall they call on him in whom they have not believed? and how shall they believe in him of whom they have not heard? and how shall they hear without a preacher?"**
> **(Romans 10:14)**

> **"So then faith cometh by hearing, and hearing by the word of God."**
> **(Romans 10:17)**

Faith for healing comes by hearing the word for healing. Preach salvation! People will be saved. Preach the baptism of the Holy Spirit! People will receive the Holy Spirit. Preach healing! People will be healed!

God said that the seed contains its ability inside itself. There are seeds that will bring forth corn because that seed is a corn seed or kernel.

The Road to Healing

"And God said, let the earth bring forth grass, the herb yielding seed, and the fruit tree yielding fruit after his kind, whose seed is in itself, upon the earth: and it was so."

(Genesis 1:11)

When you hear a healing message, you are allowing a *"healing seed"* to be planted in your spirit. It will bring forth healing. These seeds of plants and herbs were already finished before they were in the ground.

"...in the day that the Lord God made the earth and the heavens,

And every plant of the field before it was in the earth, and every herb of the field before it grew:"

(Genesis 2:4,5)

Healing belongs to you, even before it is planted in your heart. Jesus has already carried your sickness and borne your affliction.

"......Himself took our infirmities and bare our sicknesses."

(Matthew 8:17)

"How to Receive Healing"

There is no sickness greater than the Word of God. All healing begins with the Word of God. (Romans 10:17) Separate yourself from unbelief! (II Timothy 3:5) God's Word is the greatest authority! Freedom from sickness comes from knowing the truth. (John 8:32) Your *"healing seeds"* are the Scriptures on healing. (Luke 8:11) Remember, Jesus does not have less authority today to heal you than He did then. If He could speak authoritative words of healing then, His words of authority can heal you NOW!

chapter three

"The Ministry of the Laying on of Hands"

> "And when Jesus was come into Peter's house, he saw his wife's mother laid, and sick of a fever.
>
> And he touched her hand, and the fever left her: and she arose, and ministered unto them."
> **(Matthew 8:14,15)**

A Divine touch! One of the ways that healing is ministered is through the laying on of hands.

> ". . . they shall lay hands on the sick, and they shall recover."
> **(Mark 16:18)**

The Spirit of God reveals to us in His Word that the hands of a believer are consecrated holy unto the Lord.

> "I will therefore that men pray every where, lifting up holy hands, without wrath and doubting."
> **(I Timothy 2:8)**

The writer of Hebrews states:

> "For we have not an high priest which cannot be touched with the feeling of our infirmities;

"The Ministry of the Laying on of Hands"

but was in all points tempted like as we are, yet without sin."
(Hebrews 4:15)

You can touch Jesus with your needs. Jesus will touch you and make you whole! Jesus, our high priest, is the fulfillment of every Old Testament priest. In Israel, once a year, the nation came up to the tabernacle and later, to the temple on the Day of Atonement. One of the symbolic acts of the atonement was the laying on of the priest's hands upon the scapegoat. Symbolically, the sins of the people were transferred to the goat, which was then driven outside the camp; thus, removing the sins of the people outside the camp!

"And Aaron shall lay both his hands upon the head of the live goat, and confess over him all the iniquities of the children of Israel, and all their transgressions in all their sins, putting them upon the head of the goat, and shall send him away by the hand of a fit man into the wilderness:

And the goat shall bear upon him all their iniquities unto a land not inhabited: and he shall let go the goat in the wilderness."
(Leviticus 16:21,22)

God allowed the laying on of hands by the priest to take the sins from the people and to be removed from them, again, by the laying on of hands.

When Jesus laid hands on the sick, they were made well. Christ, as our Substitute, was carrying away those sickenesses in anticipation of His cross. Jesus carried our sicknesses, literally as God's scapegoat, He bore them to the cross.

"That it might be fulfilled which was spoken by Esaias the prophet, saying, Himself took our infirmities, and bare our sicknesses."
(Matthew 8:17)

Jesus fulfilled this prophecy of Isaiah before He went to the cross! Jesus was healing the sick before Calvary! He was removing diseases from the people on His journey to Calvary. Just as the scapegoat was driven outside the camp, so Christ was crucified outside of the Holy City.

Just as the scapegoat symbolically carried the sins of the people, so Christ carried all sin and sickness upon Himself. Just as the people were left free of all reproach, so we are free from all sin and infirmities. When Jesus layed hands on the sick, He was taking their infirmities. Heaven touched earth and blasted hell.
GLORY!

The laying on of hands can impart healing power. There are nine gifts of the Spirit listed in I Corinthians 12:1-11. One of these gifts is the *"gifts of healing"*.

"....to another the gifts of healing by the same Spirit."
(I Corinthians 12:9)

"The Ministry of the Laying on of Hands"

The great apostle Paul had tremendous results in getting people to receive healing. He was not a novice.

One of Paul's desires was to help people receive these wonderful, supernatural gifts of God's Spirit. The church in Rome received a letter containing this information:

> **"For I long to see you, that I may impart unto you some spiritual gift, to the end ye may be established;"**
> **(Romans 1:11)**

Spiritual gifts may be imparted or given to believers. Paul even told us one way that those gifts may be given or imparted to that one who believes God's Word!

> **"Wherefore I put thee in remembrance that thou stir up the gift of God, which is in thee by the putting on of my hands."**
> **(II Timothy 1:6)**

The gift from God that was in Timothy, came by Paul putting his hands on him! Spiritual gifts may be given by the laying on of hands. One of those gifts is the *"gifts of healing"*. Healing may be given to the one needing that gift by the laying on of hands!

JESUS LAID HANDS ON HIM TWICE

> **"And he cometh to Bethsaida; and they bring a blind man unto him, and besought him to touch him.**

The Road to Healing

And he took the blind man by the hand, and led him out of the town; and when he had spit on his eyes, and put his hands upon him, he asked him if he saw ought.

And he looked up, and said, I see men as trees, walking.

After that he put his hands again upon his eyes, and made him look up: and he was restored, and saw every man clearly."
(Mark 8:22-25)

The man came to Jesus looking for a touch. Many times in the Scripture, people asked Jesus to pray for them. Here, the man asks for a touch. The Bible says everyone that *"asketh shall receive."*

Jesus never prayed for this blind man! He spit on his eyes. The man was restored so that he could see clearly! Notice, Jesus did not spit again. He laid hands on him again!

Since the Holy Scriptures do not record Jesus praying for the man, and when the miracle was completed, the man saw clearly, God must use the laying on of hands to impart His power into our bodies.

You can receive a miracle through the laying on of hands. God will even work special miracles by the hands of His ministers.

"And God wrought special miracles by the hands of Paul:

So that from his body were brought unto the

"The Ministry of the Laying on of Hands"

sick handkerchiefs or aprons, and the diseases departed from them, and the evil spirits went out of them."
(Acts 19:11,12)

John G. Lake tells the story of how God used him in bringing a special miracle to a young man through the laying on of hands.

"Over in Indiana some years ago was a farmer who was a friend of Brother Fockler and myself. His son had been in South America and had a dreadful case of typhoid fever. He had no proper nursing and as a result, he had developed a great fever sore. It was ten inches in diameter. The whole abdomen became grown up with proud flesh; one layer on top of another layer, until there were five layers. The nurse had to lift those layers and wash it with an antiseptic to keep the maggots out of it.

When he exposed the body to me to pray for him, I was shocked. I had never seen anything like it before. As I went to pray for him, I spread my fingers out wide, and put my hand on the cursed growth of proud flesh. I prayed God in the Name of Jesus Christ to blast that curse of hell, and burn it up by the power of God. Then I took the train and came back to Chicago. The next day, I received a telegram, saying, "Lake, the most unusual thing has happened. One hour after you left, the whole print of your hand was burned into that growth a quarter of an inch deep!"

The Road to Healing

You talk about the voltage from heaven and the power of God! Why there is lightning in the soul of Jesus. The lightnings of Jesus heal men by their flesh; sin dissolves, disease flees when the power of God approaches."

Have faith in God! There is no sin that Christ's blood won't cover. There is no disease He cannot heal. Jesus wants you to be well! Christ is God's plan for ending sickness and disease!

HEALING HANDS

Healing hands reach out to me
from the Cross of Calvary.
Compassion bids my sickness go;
virtue is in that crimson flow!
Life and joy fills my soul,
Healing's song begins to roll.

Happy am I, healed and blessed,
long at last, I'm at rest.
Christ is Healer, of that I'm sure.
He'll be yours, too, friend, open the door!
Sickness and disease will vanish away,
When you experience your healing today!

- Selected

chapter four

"How to Keep Your Healing"

Jesus taught us that it is possible to lose our healing. However it is God's Will for us to keep everything that He gives to us. What must we do then to make sure that the enemy does not steal our healing?

It is possible to lose what God gives you. This is true of every blessing that He makes available to us. Jesus healed a crippled man at the pool of Bethesda. Later, when he saw him at the temple he warned the man to stay free from sin now that he was healed or a worse thing could come on him. **John 5:14**

The Bible says that, **"Discretion shall preserve thee, understanding shall KEEP thee:" Proverbs 2:11** We need to have the understanding of how to keep what the Lord gives us and this is especially true of the healing that we may receive in our mind and bodies.

I prayed for a deaf woman in Indiana some years ago. She had not heard out of either ear for over 20 years. Her son was a minister friend of mine and had asked me to pray for his mother when I was in her city.

The Road to Healing

Her other son brought her to the meeting and I prayed for her at the end of the service. Instantly, both of her ears came open and she could hear the ticking of a watch in both ears. The people praised God for it was a wonderful miracle.

They went out to go home and I began to pray for others. Five minutes later, the back door opened and the son motioned for me to come to the back of the church. I went back. He said, *"Mom locked herself in the car."* He told me that she was mad. When I asked him why he told me that both of her ears had closed and she was deaf again!

He told me on the way out of the church he said to his mother, *"Isn't it great that Jesus has healed you?"* He said that her reply was, *"I hope it lasts."* She could not keep her healing for more than 5 minutes.

The more valuable your blessing the more the devil will try to steal it from you.

The Bible teaches us that God, **"will keep the feet of his saints,"** 1 Samuel 2:9.

Then again the scriptures declare **"But the Lord is faithful, who shall stablish you, and keep you from evil."**
                              (2 Thessalonians 3:3)

"How to Keep Your Healing"

WE ARE KEPT BY GOD'S WORD

"So then faith cometh by hearing, and hearing by the word of God."
(Romans 10:17)

You need to read His Word to strengthen your faith. Doubt will rob you of healing every time. Find a promise from the Bible that has to do with what you need and build your faith on that promise. The faith that comes from this puts you in touch with Him and gives you the ability to receive and keep the very thing that you have needed.

We are kept by the HEARD WORD! Jesus spoke of the sower who sowed the seed in four kinds of ground. He said that that seed was the Word of God. You are God's good ground!

Jesus said, **"But that on the good ground are they, which in an honest and good heart, having heard the word, KEEP it, and bring forth fruit with patience,"**
(Luke 8:15)

That is why I believe that it is vitally important to go to a church where the healing word is sown. You cannot expect to keep your healing or anything God gives you if you attend a church that does not believe that the Lord heals today or that He will heal everyone that comes to Him in faith believing.

You keep your healing by getting in an atmosphere of faith created by the hearing of the Word!

WE ARE KEPT BY OUR CONFESSION

If you want to keep your healing then you must resist the devil. The devil does not want us to learn the life of faith and the Biblical laws that govern it. The enemy constantly seeks to make us fearful and cause us to doubt. I have seen where many times the devil will try to bring on us the old symptoms after we have been healed.

> "Submit yourselves therefore to God. Resist the devil, and HE WILL FLEE FROM YOU."
> **(James 4:7)**

It has been said that we rise or fall according to the level of our confession. That woman in Indiana allowed her words to reopen the door to deafness and I am sure bitterness as well. We must learn to talk back to the devil.

I love to shout that verse in **Isaiah 53:5, "But he was wounded for our transgressions, he was bruised for our iniquities: the chastisement of our peace was upon him; and with his stripes WE ARE HEALED."**

"How to Keep Your Healing"

WE ARE KEPT BY OUR PRAISE

We need to learn how to praise God by faith before and after we receive our healing. Praise Him before you see it or feel it. Then praise Him for what He has done after you receive it.

> **4 REJOICE in the Lord always: and again I say, REJOICE.**
>
> **5 Let your moderation be known unto all men. The Lord is at hand.**
>
> **6 Be careful for nothing; but in every thing by prayer and supplication with THANKSGIVING let your requests be made known unto God.**
>
> **7 And the peace of God, which passeth all understanding, shall KEEP your hearts and minds through Christ Jesus.**
> **(Philippians 4:4-7)**

Your praise can also make you whole. The things that the disease or sickness may have taken from your mind and body will be restored as you praise the Lord for His wonderful works!

Ministry Product
Order Online @ www.tedshuttlesworth.com

Books

Healing Scriptures
5 Myths About Giving
The Mighty Baptism in the Holy Spirit
There's Room At the Cross
Obedience the Key to Prosperity

CD'S

Singles

5 Myths About Giving
God's Plan For Your Life
The Anointing of Recovery
What Faith Can Do

Albums

Concerning Spiritual Gifts - 4 CD Album
Divine Healing Vol 1 - 3 CD Album
Obedience the Key to Prosperity - 3 CD Album

DVD'S

El Shaddai
How to Build a Covering for your Family
Redeemed from the Curse
The Anointing of Recovery
The Devil and the Day of Pentecost
The Miracle is in Your House

FAITH ALIVE!
A PUBLICATION OF TED SHUTTLESWORTH EVANGELISTIC ASSOCIATION

Reporting Miracle-Revival from the Auditorium and Tent Crusades across the Nation!

EACH ISSUE CONTAINS:

- A FAITH BUILDING MESSAGE
- TESTIMONIES OF OUTSTANDING MIRACLES
- CRUSADE SCHEDULE
- AND MUCH MORE ...

FREE!

BROTHER SHUTTLESWORTH, PLEASE RUSH ME THE LATEST ARTICLE OF FAITH ALIVE!

NAME: _____

ADDRESS: _____

CITY: _____ STATE: _____ ZIP: _____

PHONE: _____

TED SHUTTLESWORTH • P.O. BOX 7 • FARMINGTON, WV 26571 USA

903-520-9999